Contents

SENSUAL Scribbles

DK MARIE

This book is for the passionate souls whose hearts bleed poetry and prose.

DK Marie

Longing and Lust

She clutches her manners
Like a string of pearls
While yearning for him
To break those inhibitions
That tie and bind her desires
She needs his passions
Like fire seeks oxygen
Craving the heat
Of his fiery embrace
As her heart thrums

Be mine
Again
& again

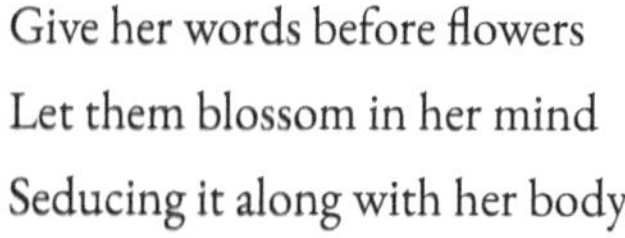

Give her words before flowers
Let them blossom in her mind
Seducing it along with her body

Offer fantasies on frosted breath
That breathes heat into her desires
Melting the burning silence
They flicker and whisper
In the amber afterglow
Of their scorching touch

His wants murmurers
Along dangerous curves
And lusty aches
Leaving love notes from him
With his mouth and body

That taunt with need
And biting passions
That leaves her
Tongue-tied in satin
Bound to touch
And his wild words

I hear the song
Of our untraveled sins
They're a graveyard of secrets
Waiting to be shared

I crave your haunting melody
It's my favorite midnight dance
Of silk and steam
That binds me in pearls of passion
Pinned beneath your kisses

Make music with me
If you dare
Let dissonant fade
And the desires
Caged in you

Free
To sing
Of our lust and love

Don't go
Or say goodbye
Stay for breakfast
Where the meal
Is you

I want more
Than tantalizing memories
And discarded dreams

Your breath mixes
With my deliberate follies
Taste the passion
Dripping from my tongue

I'm hungry
For your succulent desires
Let me dine on you

Dreaming of midnight desires
Of dark kisses between satin sheets
And between her velvet thighs
Catching her moans of pleasure
Dancing through his dreams

I'm standing before you
Burning in my sins
Do you extinguish my flame
Or are you a match
Lighting our desires
A fire to your fantasies
Blazing kisses to my pleasure

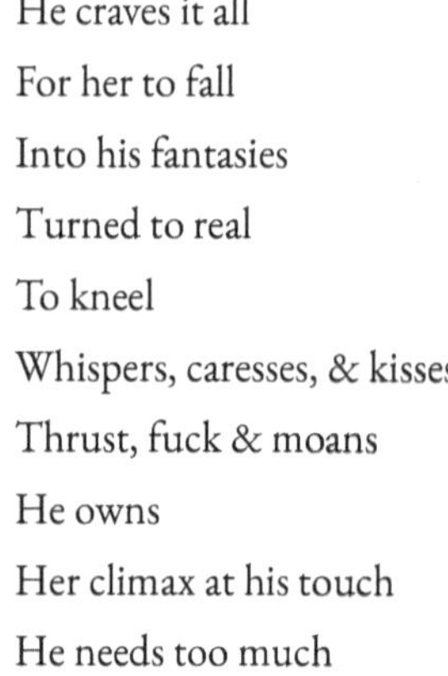

He craves it all

For her to fall

Into his fantasies

Turned to real

To kneel

Whispers, caresses, & kisses

Thrust, fuck & moans

He owns

Her climax at his touch

He needs too much

I sleep to dream of you

Trying to discover

If you're my dream man

Just a fantasy

With the smile of an angel

And the mind of a demon

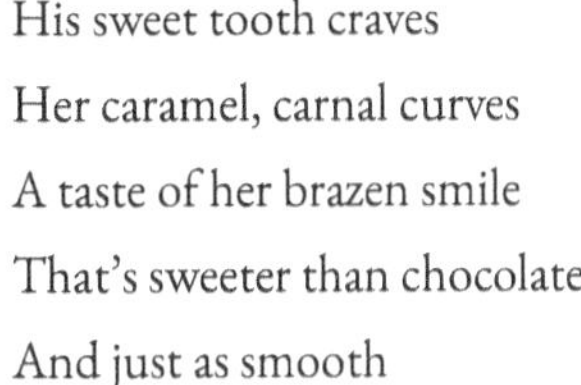

His sweet tooth craves
Her caramel, carnal curves
A taste of her brazen smile
That's sweeter than chocolate
And just as smooth

She radiates sugarplum passion
Melting all his inhibitions and restraints
He's waiting, counting the hours
To taste her sugar-coated kisses

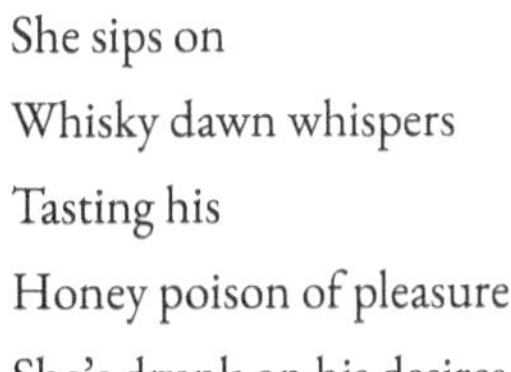

She sips on
Whisky dawn whispers
Tasting his
Honey poison of pleasure
She's drunk on his desires

Loving the way bliss burns
As it and she goes down
Tasting his passion and pleasure

In light of the gleam
In his eyes
That takes me by surprise
I have a confession
Where told lies
Wither and die
On Aphrodite's pen
That drips with longing
And a sense of belonging
Coating my skin with lust
As she writes our love letters
On silk sensuality

I'm head over heels
It all holds so much appeal

Playing with your angels and demons
Immersed in your carnal fires
Drowning in your desires

Will you be my midnight kiss
That shatters the quiet of night
As you and the moon
Unravel my passion
Wrapping me in sweet sins
And a weave of star lust
From dusk to dawn
Let me treasure this dream
Sheathed in one more hour of lust
Before you must
Let me go

He's her favorite dessert
-such a flirt
The pale splash of passion
-something she can't ration
A salted caramel sip of sin
-makes her grin
Insatiable tangling thighs
-and hungry eyes
They're speaking tongues
-hearts beating like drums
As she takes a bite
-everything feels so right

Insatiable desires drip drama
Rustling— a ruffle from the rift
Where her passions part and pull
And darkness calls to depravities
That tug on the ropes and rapture
Of tantalizing temptations
The seductive stage is set
She's ready to please, to play her part

I'm tied up in knots
Twisted in a sedate slump
Needing you tonight
To unbind my tension
Burn the bridge
Between right and wrong
Releasing your savage storm
To rain on me
Your salacious sins
Until I'm wet
With delicious desires
Hold me, pin me
With your passion
Tie me in knots

She prays
For sunset atonement
Were sins aren't forgiven

But given
Under the cathedral
Of the moon and stars
Where the chaotic sea
Of her heart is calmed
Upon the alter
of his body

I lost tonight
And perhaps tomorrow
imprisoned with thoughts of him
This is my naked guilt
A signed confession
Whispered against his skin

My only wish
Is for my last breath
To be a final kiss
Against his lips and love

I'll be fine
With any punishment dealt
Because the true crime

Is existing without his touch
It's never enough
I'm sentenced to a life
Of craving him

In a paradoxical dream
On an ephemeral night
She shares the sky
With an intimate mystery
That is him

They're on the far side of hello
So close to goodbye
His kiss fades with the stars

She picks the fantasy of forever
Over the dawning reality
That he'll disappear
With the moon

She's alone
Dreaming
Dripping with expectations
Fantasizing
Dipping, melting at sensations
Remembering
His sensual touch

Her   Lust
Amour
&   Passion
Are a menagerie
Locked & hidden
Behind a fog
Of faulty virtue
& false modesty

His lingering touch

& wicked smile
Was the key
That unlocked her cage
Freeing her desires

Between the softness
Of her kinky kisses
And the hardness
Of his dark desires
Waits their fortune
A teasing treasure
Of so much pleasure

Call me
Whisper and breathe
Tell me all your needs

And hot, dark desires
Through the telephone wires
Twist, tie, and bind
My mind
To your words and cravings
Have me misbehaving
Pleading, screaming, & kneeling
For you

His frenzied tenderness
Is treacherous
It takes her to unbearable heights
Sometimes it bites
Other times it soothes
Making her crave all his moves
As he tackles new heights
And fills her with his delights

Penetrate her veil
Find her secret desires
Run your hands along her soft dreams

Taste her pulsating power and ecstasy

She's a delicate delight
Never fails to ignite
His little flirt
Is such a sweet dessert
Her flavor is desire and lust
Together they thrust, ready to combust
Until sated, languid on frenzied fulfillment

My transparent transgressions
Slip and slide, defile
Along his dangerous smile
The flash of teeth and tongue
Is that extra something
That brings a fluttering

Of demanding desires
Ending in fiery sighs

Give me a bouquet
Of your kinky corruptions
Let me inhale
Intoxicating, titillating touches
As sensual stimulating scents
Unfolds my petals of passion
Watch me flourish and bloom
Under the sweet perfume
Of your desires

You're a closed book
A virtual story

I'm intent on reading
So please open
Your pages
To me
I promise
To savor
Your flavor
And enjoy
Every divine line

Here you are
Next to me
Hungry for games
So why don't you
Toy with me

I'll sip on you
Tasting our forever
It's the flavor of passion
That'll never satiate
My hunger for you
But we'll have fun trying

Are you ready
To play?

Lasting Love

I travel, I search
For what, I don't know

A new life, adventure,
Understanding, inner serenity
Love, a little lust

I find bits and pieces
Of myself all over the world

In stranger's eyes
In kind smiles
Even in their cons & shams

I travel, I find
For what, I now know

In a village in the middle of lost America
I sit in the corner of the cafe
Writing poetry that tastes of you
I sip on warm memories
Of lust, love, and longing
It's a bitter brew
That's somehow sweet

Wrapped around her

Contempt and cold
Behold her
The red-hot passion

Are you bold
Enough to melt her
Find hidden compassion
And hold her

She surrounds herself with his broken
Not because she fracted for more
Too heartbroken

They lean on each other
Becoming less alone
To another

Carrying shattered pieces
Mended souls
Masterpieces

I wasn't free
Until I chained
Myself to you

The remedy for
My wandering soul
Was staying with you

Sincerely yours,
Forever

Beautiful words
Fall from your lips
As if our love
Was written in the stars
Along the ink of the moon
And the shadows of the stars
Spilling across the sky

In a constellation of passion

The warning signs
All point to
Playing it safe
But new adventures
Sing to our
Bookmarked hearts
Let's lose our place
Jump to the next chapter
Where love's the copilot
Take me away
Where passion is wild
And carefree
We'll move mountains
Chase oceans
Live our favorite story

Addicted to you
To the taste of us
The lick of secret sensations
And swallow of private passions
The compulsive craving
For our lasting love
Makes me wanton and weak
Strong in my hopeful heart

She dove
Fearing the fall
Of what he'd break

Echoes of pain faded
Wrapped in his love
Cocooned from sorrow

Her unanchored breathes
Settle into him
Her hollow heart

Fills with his devotion
Healing all wounds

Love grows here
Between knowledge
And intuition
They're entwined
In words and hearts
That echoes on paper

A poem to him
Is the key to his heart
It unlocks passions
And whispers
Eternally yours

In a blur of headlights
And wild nights
We crash
Burn inhibitions to ash
A collision of time
We feel so fine
Together
All lace and leather
Fire and ice
Far from nice
A taste of unconditional
Nothing traditional
This love and lust
That I trust
With you
Feels so true

His gaze covers
My unsettled flesh
Reaching toward
My heart of glass
It shatters against the force
Of his knowing smile

As he reads me
All my fears and desires
Yet he still loves
My story

Love grows
Between knowledge
And intuition
They're entwined
In words and hearts
That echoes on paper
And souls

A poem penned for him
Is the key to his heart
It unlocks passions

And whispers
Eternally yours

Your musical voice
is a catalyst
My tripping words
find your rhythm
Our waltzing heartbeats
dance to a song
of Love

Roped tongues tangled
Entwined in a kiss
A breath
Breathing a wish
Whispering

A moonlit melody
That's more than
Just a love song
It's symphony
Sung in the colors of love
Singing desire
Devotion
Upon every wishing star

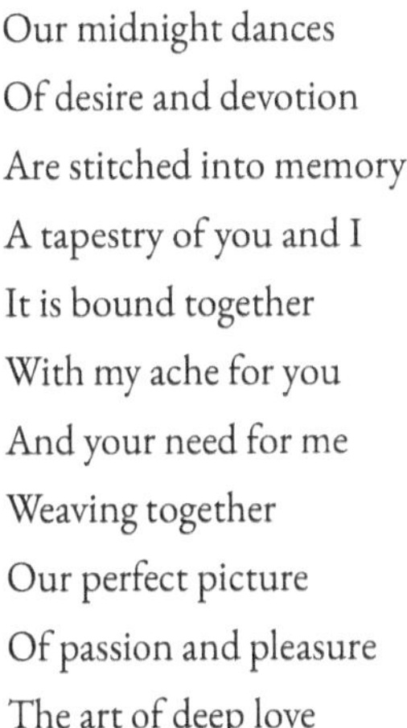

Our midnight dances
Of desire and devotion
Are stitched into memory
A tapestry of you and I
It is bound together
With my ache for you
And your need for me
Weaving together
Our perfect picture
Of passion and pleasure
The art of deep love

Hold
Our love
Delicate, like snowflakes
In your hand

Melting inhibitions
And my heart

Release me
To roam
Through passion
Pain and persistence

Hold me
As we feel our way
To every fantasy
Finding forever

Kiss me like
You mean it
or let me
Go

Of today and yesterday
Before dawn breaks
And early morning dreams rise
Our love travels among the missing
Wounded but alive
Searching through stardust memories
Those priceless riches
Will light the way
Back into each other's arms

She's hopelessly intertwined
Lost, following heady traces
Of forest-scented love

She's on his heated trail
Where passion flows
And his ethereal touch

Lights her
Way to wild lust
Where vines of passion
Wrap around her lost heart

I didn't believe
Your beautiful face
And the magic
In your fingers and fantasies
Belonged to my feral flesh

Simply wishes
Between worlds and wants

You opened your eyes
And all your passions
Were laid bare
And I saw
Your desire
Was mine

There was a covenant
Of hope between them

It began with a twilight of tears
And her cries
As tormenting memories
And emotions
Spilled from her past
Staining her future

He held her in the now
And midnight reveries
Becoming her North star
Guiding the way
To their love

I give him credit
His patience & passion
Are priceless

Slivers of painful memories
Try to press me down
Onto my demons
Making me shutter & shake

But so does he
Pausing the words
My whole world quiets
As I focus on the now
Where his enchanting desires
Seduce my hidden soul

This token of his love
Offers pockets of peace
Amongst all the sorrow

I hold my breath
On the precipice
Then fully breathe
As the scent of you
Draws me in

To our secret garden

It's wild and dangerous
But you love the bite
Of my thorns
And laying on my bed
Of roses
As my petals hold you
In the agony of ecstasy

Buried deep inside me
Is your seed
It blooms in my heart
And flourishing fantasies

Written on the flood
Of desires
That pollinates my passions
Is our immortal words
Of blossoming devotion

We'll grow together
Never to leave
This field of euphoria

She worships
His Sunday love
As he prays
For her sins
The script of life
Is torn and twisted
Sheets between them
His hands rewrite
Their story
Fallen words
Land in her heart
Whispered promises
Of be mine
Have changed them
Filling her soul
With pages of him
Their epic love story

I fell for your wayward smile
We came together
With a bang

I asked for too much
You gave your all
As I begged
Do not be gentle

Your bad
Is my good time
The wrong
That feels right

You understand
My silent language
That sings
Your wish is mine
To hold & love
Until the end
Of us

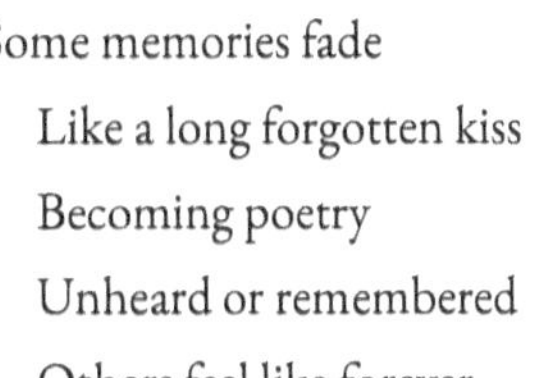

Some memories fade
    Like a long forgotten kiss
    Becoming poetry
    Unheard or remembered
    Others feel like forever

Remaining still & strong
A love letter
Tattooed on my heart
Tied in a bow around my soul
Shining bright
Stars holding
My secret wishes
& our story

Only with his permission
And that single word
Strip
Do her inhibitions cave
And she begins to crave
The fire of his kiss
She tastes forever together
In the indulgence
That's the power of love
From his lips

You play my strings
Like a harp
I dance to your desires
Twirl to the tantalizing timbre
Of your persistent passions
I take a leap of faith
Over this chasm of love
Without a worry
Distance doesn't matter
I'll land in your arms
And kiss every throbbing inch
Of your hammering heart

She's a woman
Of masks & mysteries
Her raven heart hides
With umbra, penumbra,

And antumbra
They keep her
In the shadows
Her hidden nature
Is ink between darkness
Yet she crafts a trail
With her desires & devotion
Hope he'll read her story
& find a way to her
Happily-Ever-After

Tripping words
Scraped lies
She's beaten and bruised
Running from love
To chase away
The ache and agony

She slows, stopping
For the gentle flutter
Of his kind heart

He kisses away hurt
Heals hope
In love
Once lost
Now found
In his soothing
Embrace

North, South, East, or West
It doesn't matter where I am
You are my world—my home
For your words are my breath
They give me love and life
For I know between your dreams
And the stars
You'll give me the moon
And a map to your heart
Where I'll reside in its shelter
Forevermore

Pride is set aside

For the ritual of roses

A promise of devotion

Has set this in motion

Kisses on my neck

Bring me to my knees

Hesitation disappears

Into a puddle of want

Taunt my petals of desire

They'll blossom and bloom

Heartbreak and Hurt

He is the reason she aches

Reliving all those mistakes

She wants to forget

His touch, his words

But need brings her to her knees

Begging, please

Reaching, grabbing for his ghost

A phantom, long gone
A shadow threat
The only thing real is her regret

She shouldn't indulge in his wicked ways
He's liable to betray
Yet, she'll stay
Because her desires refuse to leave
They're ready to receive
His mix of pleasure and pain
That rains
A combination of love and hate
That sates
Her needs
But her heart bleeds

Even if
The tears and pain

Had foreshadowed

I wouldn't abstain

I'd still have traveled

The insane

Path that ended

In vain

With heartbreak

Tasting of cheap champagne

If it meant loving you

My heart and bane

Will you love her, for her
And not who you want her to be?

Say you love her, then walk away
Tell her she's worth so much
Just not enough

My heart aches

It breaks

For all I desire

And the way l conspire

To set my life on fire

I watch it burn

As yearn

For the flame

That maims

My soul

Yet has control

She's tired of kneeling

In shame before perfection

Begging for affection

Her twisted and mangled pieces

Fit her just fine

Devine

There is a unique beauty

In the broken & cracked
Heart's intact

I miss you, I want you
But I don't need you
Take me, Use me
Just don't abuse me

I miss you
Or perhaps the fantasy of you

Not the reality of us
And the cold truth of us

My broken bits turn from you
We are no longer
Me and you

It is just
Me
and
You

The contours of my heart
Have an unnatural sag &dip
It's a lonely hollow vessel
Where the only sound
Is the echo of tears
And the chaos of angry whispers

Your betrayal has opened my eyes
I see the deceptive smiles and so many lies
Hear the hollow tinny of your laughter

The false Happily-Ever-Afters
And know your velvet touch covers a hard heart
That is so willing to tear me apart

I'm watching you
Watch her
And I finally saw
What I didn't want to see
Persistent perspicacity
Cannot be ignored
I'm looking for love
You've looked away
Closed your eyes to me
But mine are open
I'm no longer blinded
By blind loveless love

He dreamed of her
Desolate beauty
How her touch
Pulled him under
Drowning in her
Oceans of love
And lust
She's is air
His kiss of life
Even as he's engulfed
In her sea of sensations

The primal instinct
To dance has dissolved
Our song is subdued
Your maestro's harmony dims
The vivace vibrations
Of our passions slow
The ivory strain
Of your body
Against mine
Has eased

A new melody
Washes over me
A cascade of goodbyes
Our melodramatic outro
Fades into memory

As the unstitched seams
Of our love fray and break
The illusion of us
Goes up in flames
Only smoke and mirrors remain
Of our heartless rhapsody
Its capricious melody
Is swallowed in the ocean's anthem
Of mistakes and regrets
That drowns passion
Unraveling out song

I should be afraid
Knowing everything
Becomes ash and dust
Including our hearts
and hopes
It is fragile poetry
And pearls

I find myself holding
Tighter to him
And these chains
That binds our liberation
As we love
With all we have
Before it's gone

In his arms
Love wrapped around them

And two become one
As desire bloomed
In their embrace

They forgot to nourish
Passion and patience
Devotion wilted
Weeds of conflict
Choked affection

They're a melancholy moment
Fading in the garden
Of wasted words
And broken promises

In the lonely sky
Of love and lust
He was her star
She wished upon
Together as one

But he forgot to remember
Their dreams & desires

She begged him
Not to let go
Of the forever feeling
But new became old

They no longer shine bold
His devotion dimmed
And her nights are dark

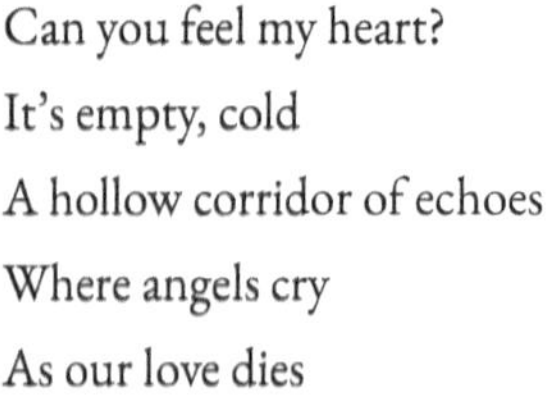

Can you feel my heart?
It's empty, cold
A hollow corridor of echoes
Where angels cry
As our love dies

We've become forgotten history
Where I am yours
But you are not mine

Just another broken morning
My pieces shatter, scatter
Cutting into my days and nights

Time and again

Our love spins

I'm dizzy and defeated

Feel cheated

I'll miss

Your kiss

But you've worn me down

I'll drown

Become a slave

If I once again forgave

I will no longer try

Goodbye

Between the ink and stars

Blood and ash

Sitting on the dusty shelves
Of life and death
Is the story of us

It's twisted together
With flirtations and fantasies
Bound by longing and lust

There are pages
Of sun-drenched morning
Paragraphs heated
By afternoon delights
Chapters inscribed
In sapphire evenings

Every line is inked
And stains our hearts
With hope and sorrow
Love and loss
Us

If you were mine

It'd be divine
But you're not

Take your useless apologies
And torpid love
My heart whispers and roars
For so much more

I want tongued confessions
Of devotion
And a little more emotion
A touch of valet sin
On my heated skin

No more tepid passions
But raging lust and trust
That lights the embers in my veins
Catching my fields of desire
Becoming a wildfire

He's dragging out the darkness
Drowning in the night
Stealing stars & tears

She's searching
Through cinders & sparks
& all the things never said
Looking for another chance at hello

In her loving palms
She holds crushed hearts
Piecing together
Their honeysuckle dreams

Coffee shop conversations
Taste of missing you
And of some concocted reality
Where I still sit on that pedestal
You placed me on
Where you kiss me now
And the bitter flavor of later
Doesn't burn my heart

Alone in the dark

Tears will fall

On empty promises

As I bank on memories

Of what was

And what will never be

They stir forgotten joys

I should bury or burn

Yet my barbed wire heart

Still bleeds

Of all the things you said

And I wish to tell you

They're careful whispers

Across my back

Secrets of a priceless

Worthless love

That broke me

I might have romanticized

His alluring sparkling eyes
That burned like wild, hot fire
So full of desire
A consuming, crazy love
That so many write of
But it was a lie
The flame flickered & died
His lively spirit
I can no longer hear it
It's now a lonely ghost
Of what was almost

How am I blindsided again?
By this pain
I've traveled this well-worn path
Done the math
The answer is always the same
Only have myself to blame

I'm feeling so old
No longer bold

As sorrow coats my smile

With denial

It's bitter

Yet sweet

This street

Of heartbreak

That makes me ache

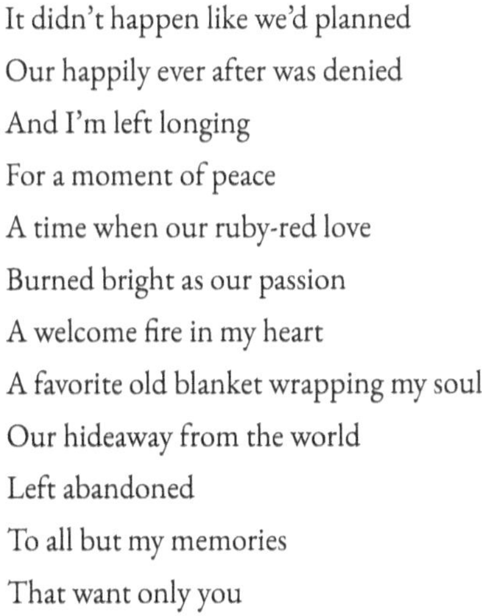

It didn't happen like we'd planned

Our happily ever after was denied

And I'm left longing

For a moment of peace

A time when our ruby-red love

Burned bright as our passion

A welcome fire in my heart

A favorite old blanket wrapping my soul

Our hideaway from the world

Left abandoned

To all but my memories

That want only you

Her love's in a mournful sleep
Wakes parched, thirsty for passion
But that was in another life
Now she only holds
Words of sorrow
That has become
Scribbled wishes in charcoal
Dark as her broken heart
They're letters to her soul
Of chapters never finished
A story left untold

The lambert love
In your eyes
Has darkened and dimmed
Between your heart and mine

There's no more yesterdays
Worth remembering or revisiting
When the body of our love
Is ash and memories
Caught in a cold wind
Of visions violated
Forever lost
In the broken promise
Of tomorrow

Pour me another
Fake fantasy
Of imagined feelings
I'll sip on his slipping stare
Stumble and fall
Between his whisky smile
Falling for his sweet talk
That'll lay sour
On my cooling skin
I'm drunk on disaster
Pour me another

Her pleas for more
Fall on deaf ears
She leaves behind
The bitter taste of goodbye
Falling into his story
Of lemonade skies
And sugar kisses
That lit up her day & night
Is an electric buzz
That burns the pages
Of her past
Opening her future
Their desires
Is such a novel feeling

I'm your part-time fantasy
All you desire from dusk to dawn
Becoming a discarded toy
From sunrise to sunset
I've let your scorpion kiss
Invade and poison my passions
For too long
It's time to search
New horizons
Finding an antidote
To the venom
Of your desires

Today she found
Lipstick stains of red
From the thorns of yesterday
They cut the fragility
Of her weeping petals
Bleeding betrayal
And broken dreams

We belong together
But you're searching
For the wonder you've lost
If you'd hold me close
You'd see it's between us

I need you closer
Than the discontent
You choose to hold
It grasps you tight

Pushing us apart
Now you're too far
Away to touch

You'll miss me
When I'm gone

I'll go

Waves of sadness crash
On the secluded shore
Of ebbing passion
Remnants of love
Are buried deep
In an ocean of sorrow

Loneliness isn't what it used to be

Lingering thoughts bloom
Breaking against hope & heartache
As we keep treading on maybes
While slowly drowning
In despair

My memory howls
It growls

Of a time in your arms
And all its charms
It's a morning dew cocktail
That's all male
A mixture of devotion & desire
That takes me higher

I was drunk on your love
It's like something from above
I'm addicted to your taste
Without it, life's a waste

Living has lost its flavor
There's nothing left to savor
Come, let's have another round
Let me drown
In my sorrow
Of no tomorrows
With you
I'm blue

Your rum lips
Taste of broken lies

I'll burn your memory
In bourbon and my spirit
I was wasted on you
But now I'm sober

What you want
I refuse to swallow
Our love is tainted
Reeking of petrol papers & cigars
Aflame with hot rage
And bad choices

I don't owe you
My tab was paid
In pain and misery
Of your broken devotion

Dreams of my soul
Are found in a dusty diary
On a forgotten shelf of my past
It's filled with spilled ink of my soul
Pages of heartbreak and passion

And passages of an old love song
I love to hum when thinking of you

Our passionate melody
Is now impassioned whispers of anger
Love has become our prison
Where our history won't help our present
It is time to face the music
We're just another song of goodbye
And I'm singing it for you

I was safe
In your cocoon
Until breaking out
Show my colors
Spreading delicate, fragile wings

Now they're crushed

Under broken promises

And the angry winds of our words

Miscellaneous Musings

For years I ran

To destinations anywhere

Searching for any place but here

Drowning in a cacophony

Of doubt and timidity

But now I'm standing

At the crossroad
Of my fractured fears
And demanding desires
Ready to adapt, to mutate
To dominate

Writing is telling the truth
In a tangle of lies

Life is living in a tangle of lies
Searching for the truth.

Take me deeper
Into your soulful depths
Where the music in your voice
Blooms velvet flirtations
And blossoms into tomorrow's secrets

Where split smiles
Pour through rays of light & dark
Matching your heart
Offering peace within
As chaos rages
In this moment of solitude
Between You and I

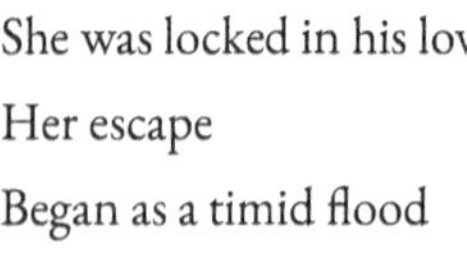

She was locked in his love
Her escape
Began as a timid flood
Drowning her todays

Until she was kissed
By lightning and longing
Of tomorrows passions

The thunder of desires
Opened the key to her heart
And a storm of eternal dreams
Flooded her future

She's more than

curves and a pretty face

She's a woman of substance

Of timeless dreams

And fearless freedom

His diva

Her mother

Their friend

The embodiment of poetry

Perseverance and passion

That blooms between stars

And shines like the sun

Lighting the way

To love and life

She's no one's Babygirl
Needs no Daddy
But a man
Of fiery desires
And piercing eyes
Who sees
She's all woman

A hopeless romantic
Sits in the distant future
At the end of the beginning
Just beyond the veil
Of what is & what was
Reading the opaque, torn pages
Of a love story
Written in her soul's shadow
Waiting for devotion & passion
To bind along her spine
Eager for that chapter
To begin

Behind her ear
That hears whispers
Of pain and passion
Sits a flower
With the scent of midnight tryst
And little white lies
Upon her skin

She counts the petals
Into piles of
He loves me
He loves me not
To finally
I love me

I see your mask
& misdirection
Sense much undulating

Below the surface
Of your sinful smile
I'm dancing with fire
Entwined with your desire
Holding smoky hearts
I'll get burned
But have an addiction
That tastes like you

Maybe next time
No, not even then
They'll never win

Her indomitable spirit
Won't ever fade
She's not afraid

Other's colorless rainbow
Will never dull her glow
Her ocean heartbeats
Will never cease

Surrender to her love
She'll satiate your soul
Make you whole

He's chasing another storm
Through the moonlight madness
His echoes of regrets
Thunder through the night
Pleading to the saints, sinners & stars
For romance & redemption
Searching for her lingering touch
She's a lighthouse in his dark
A beacon of passion & pain

His poetic melodies
Are sugarplum dreams
That sing

Between the shadows & me
Dulling the prolonged agony
Telling a story
Each chapter
Heals my tempest heart
That was betrayed by love
The tenderness of his song
Is written in devotion & adoration
That mends my wounded soul

We walk our path
To our faceless future
It's no Garden of Eden
There's twists and turns
Sneaky shadows
Trying to steal our sun
I'll get lost
Flowers will distract you
We'll learn love has thorns
But also that it's gentle
As a kiss from a rose

Whoever said darkness

Holds dreariness

Never played

With the thoughts

In my head

Because waiting

On the other side

Of the moon

Are kaleidoscope dreams

Coloring the night

Embracing my heart

Saturating every breath

With the taste of fantasies

Midnight chocolate

And lingering lust

The long journey
East
Entering at the end
But ready to begin
West
Waiting for desires
To soothe our fires
South
Sanity lost in screams
Chasing our dreams
North
Near, counting the hours
Under love's power
We found our way
Today

Willing to play
The hand I was dealt
Reap the rewards
Suffer the losses

Offering sorrow & desires
In this long journey
Of hope & despair
Chasing dreams
Just out of reach
Because I know
At the end
I'm the master
Of my game

What makes life
Is in the eye
Of the beholder
Some crave
Reason and reality
Others fantastic fantasies

Mine is an elegant balance
That tend to tip
When I wake
My sleeping demons
For he is my muse

And laying beneath
In restless slumber
Stroking my chaos
Awakening mayhem

I permit his entrance
There's no choice in the matter
For in the static dark unfolding
There is the intimate joining
Of imagination and inspiration
There is so much wonder
In his visceral visions
When I let him inside me

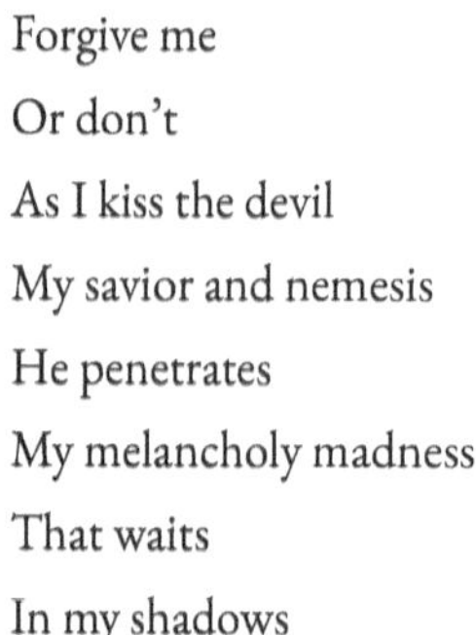

Forgive me
Or don't
As I kiss the devil
My savior and nemesis
He penetrates
My melancholy madness
That waits
In my shadows

Releasing my final words
Or pleasure and pain
Come
You want - You need
The risk and release
Of this seductive story

His second-hand kisses
Are haunting threads of mayhem
That taxi in her mind
Hitching a ride
With chaos and pandemonium
Driving desires to her wanton core
Crashing into passion
It's a head-on collision
Of poor decisions and prurience
That'll hurt
But the pain's worth the pleasure

Stay up all night
Exploring my galaxies
Tasting my succulent stars

Trace my constellations
Of tattooed memories
That has guided us here

Eclipse my mind and passions
Bind me to your Milky Way
As I dip into your desires

You're my cosmos
And I'm the light
On your darkest night

The tart taste of games
Is a study in red

As anger becomes passion

His strategic moves
Is attempting to play
With her emotions

A checkmate delivered
By the Queen
Has the King
F
a
l
l
i
n
g
for her

He's a snake
His love was hate
An acid, a poison

That tried to destroy

But wild roses grow
Within her soul
They cling & climb
Turning venom
Into an elegant failure

Despite his attempt
To pick & pluck
At tender beauty
Her resistant heart
Continues to bloom

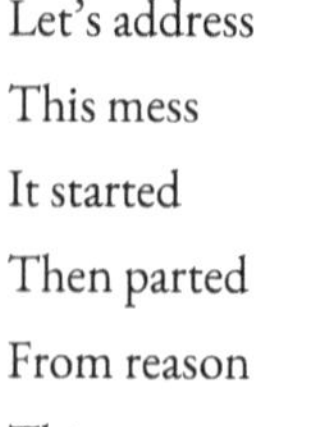

Let's address
This mess
It started
Then parted
From reason
This crazy season

Our whiskey adventure

A venture
Of love and lust
That tumbled and thrust
Us into a mess

Lets address, confess
We should have passed
But it was a blast...

The hangover
Nearly knocked over
Our life into strife
Pulled us down
And around
To reckless fun

But I'll run
Toward it again
Because I gain
A buzz like no other
There's no another
Only you

She craves his nectar
His sensual, animal grace
It makes her ache
Burn for him
He enters her like heat
A mysterious dream
They take flight
Aware the delicious bliss won't last
Their rapture and reverie is fragile
As the wings of a bee
That stings

Seasons change
we acquiesce
Summer to winter
dispatching memories
Of warm skin
under a glowing sun
Flowers and love
perfuming the air
Fireflies dancing at dusk

Like flickering candles
Porchlight glowing
calling us home

Burnt Brandy nights
Quench my parched passions
Warming my wanton ways
The usurper of my sins
I'm drunk on your desires
Willing to swallow and savor
Your sweet seductions

Afterword

Thank you for reading. Reviews have a huge impact on authors. Leaving one where you got this book or whatever review site you love is appreciate them so much- word of mouth is our bread, butter, and honey! Even a simple sentence would mean the world to me.

Thank you!

DK Marie

Also By DK Marie

I am a voracious reader and writer. Besides this poetry book, I have written six contemporary romance novels that are filled with heart, heat, and a kiss of humor. They are brimming with confident heroines and kind heroes, all living, loving, and lusting in and around my hometown of Detroit, Michigan.

If you'd like to learn more about her romance novels, keep turning the pages :-)

LAKE HOUSE LOVE series

https://dkmarie.com/books-2/

In a world where love is often rushed and superficial, in the Lake House Love series, you'll meet heroes who redefine what it means to be a true gentleman – they will steal your heart, one kind gesture and heated kiss at a time.

In these standalone novels, you'll meet characters marked by their past and haunted by their emotional scars. They are beautifully flawed, and their wounds, like battle scars, become their source of strength. Witness how their shared journey of healing and self-discovery will ignite a connection rooted not only in desire but also in genuine emotion and understanding.

From the first page to the last, these stories weave together elements of heat, heart, and humor, creating a rich tapestry of emotions that will tug at your heartstrings. You'll find yourself charmed by the witty banter and the playful dynamics between the characters, all while experiencing the emotional rollercoaster of their journey.

https://dkmarie.com/books-2/

Opposites Attract is a sensational standalone romance series where insta-lust ignites into an inferno of undeniable attraction. Brace yourself for a pulse-pounding tale of imperfectly perfect heroes fueled by equal measures of scorching heat and irresistible heart.

You'll meet characters so enchantingly flawed they'll steal your breath away. With a magnetic pull that defies reason, their chemistry sizzles from the very first encounter, leaving you breathless at every turn. Lose yourself in their journey as they navigate a tempestuous sea of desire, willing to risk it all for a taste of forbidden passion.

Our heroes are not your typical knights in shining armor; they are refreshingly flawed, with shattered hearts that yearn to be healed. Prepare for love stories that embrace their vulnerability and prove that true love finds a way, even with complete opposites.